Arranged by **DAN COATES**

S0-ARK-734

TWO THUMBS UP!

TODAY'S GREAT MOVIE SONGS

FOR THE ELEMENTARY STUDENT

Project Manager: Carol Cuellar

Dan Coates

One of today's foremost personalities in the field of printed music, Dan Coates has been providing teachers and professional musicians with quality piano material since 1975. Equally adept in arranging for beginners or accomplished musicians, his Big Note, Easy Piano and Professional Touch arrangements have made a significant contribution to the industry.

Born in Syracuse, New York, Dan began to play piano at the age of four. By the time he was 15, he'd won a New York State competition for music composers. After high school graduation, he toured the United States, Canada and Europe as an arranger and pianist with the world-famous group Up With People.

Dan settled in Miami, Florida, where he studied piano with Ivan Davis at the University of Miami while playing professionally throughout southern Florida. To date, his performance credits include appearances on "Murphy Brown" and "My Sister Sam" and at the Opening Ceremonies of the 1984 Summer Olympics in Los Angeles. Dan has also accompanied such artists as Dusty Springfield and Charlotte Rae.

In 1982, Dan began his association with Warner Bros. Publications—an association that has produced more than four hundred Dan Coates books and sheets. Throughout the year, he conducts piano workshops nationwide, during which he demonstrates his popular arrangements.

Contents

A WHOLE NEW WORLD
(From Walt Disney's "ALADDIN")

Words by
TIM RICE

Music by
ALAN MENKEN
Arranged by DAN COATES

Moderate, steady tempo

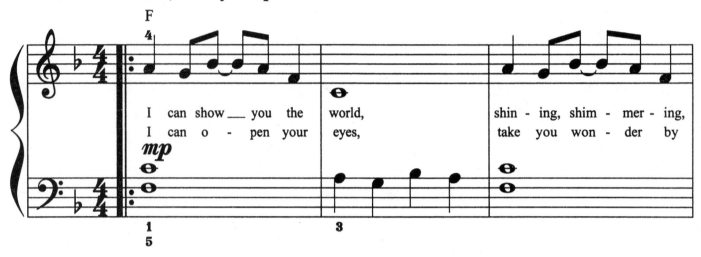

I can show ___ you the world,
I can o - pen your eyes,
shin - ing, shim - mer - ing,
take you won - der by

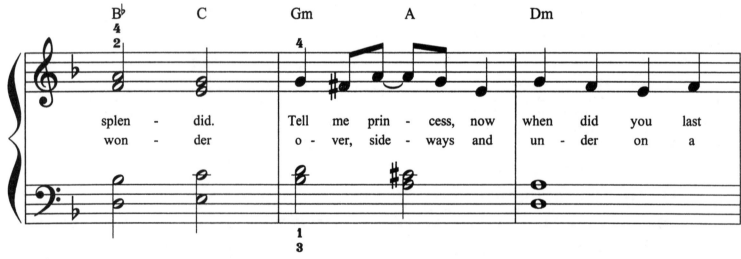

splen - did.
won - der
Tell me prin - cess, now
o - ver, side - ways and
when did you last
un - der on a

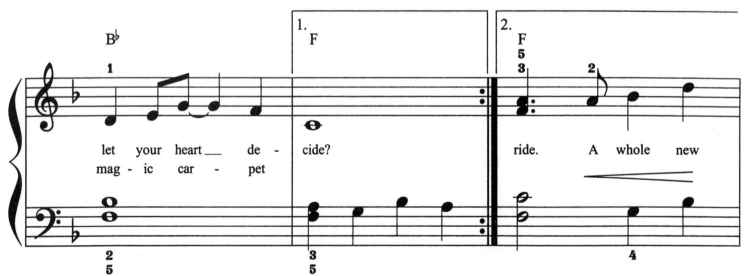

let your heart ___ de - cide?
mag - ic car - pet
ride.
A whole new

6

COUNT ON ME

Words and Music by
BABYFACE, WHITNEY HOUSTON
and **MICHAEL HOUSTON**
Arranged by DAN COATES

Count on me __ through thick and thin, a friend - ship that __ will nev - er end. When you are weak, __ I will be strong, help - ing you __ to car - ry on. __ Call on me, __ I will be there. Don't be a - fraid.

Count on Me - 3 - 1

Featured in the M-G-M Picture "THE WIZARD OF OZ"

WE'RE OFF TO SEE THE WIZARD

(The Wonderful Wizard of Oz)

Lyric by
E.Y. HARBURG

Music by
HAROLD ARLEN
Arranged by DAN COATES

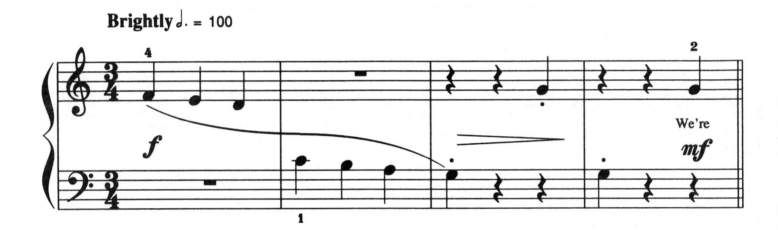

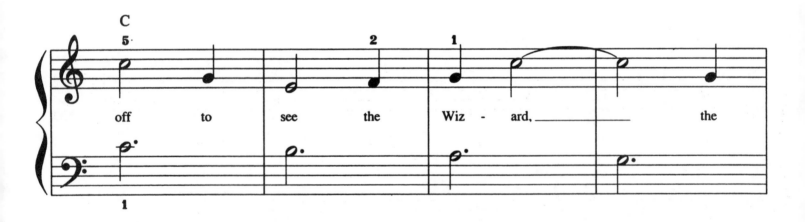

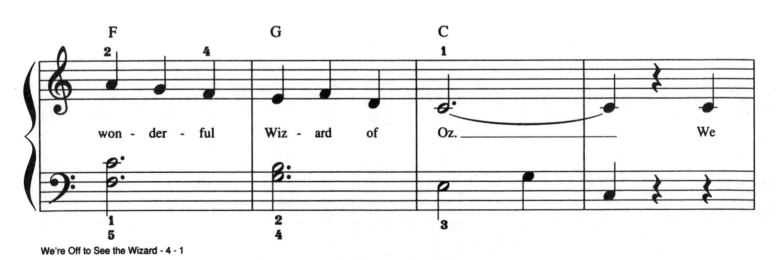

We're Off to See the Wizard - 4 - 1

THEME FROM ICE CASTLES
(Through the Eyes of Love)

Lyrics by
CAROLE BAYER SAGER

Music by
MARVIN HAMLISCH
Arranged by DAN COATES

Slowly, with expression

Please, don't let this feel - ing end. It's ev - 'ry - thing I am, ev - 'ry - thing I
now, I can take the time. I can see my life as it comes up

want to be.
shin - ing now.
I can see what's
Reach - ing out to
mine now,
touch you,

16

side me, I'm al - right.

Coda

through   the   eyes _____ of   love.

rit. e dim.

Please don't let this feeling end.
It might not come again
And I want to remember
How it feels to touch you
How I feel so much
Since I found you
Looking through the eyes of love.

From the Twentieth Century Fox Motion Picture
"ANASTASIA"

AT THE BEGINNING

Lyrics by
LYNN AHRENS

Music by
STEPHEN FLAHERTY
Arranged by DAN COATES

Moderate rock ballad

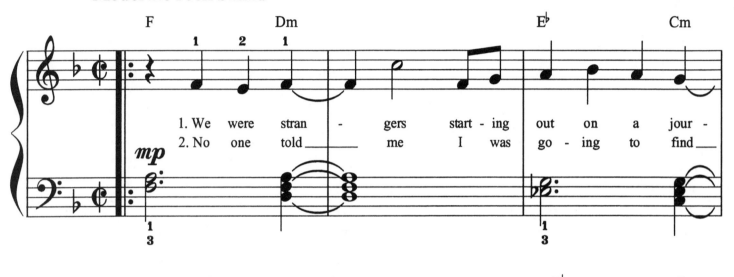

1. We were stran - gers start - ing out on a jour -
2. No one told ___ me I was go - ing to find ___

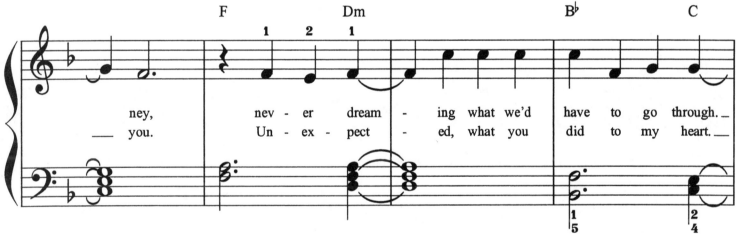

ney, nev - er dream - ing what we'd have to go through. ___
you. Un - ex - pect - ed, what you did to my heart. ___

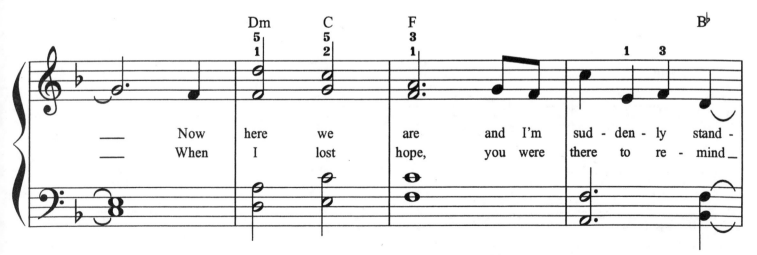

___ Now here we are and I'm sud - den - ly stand -
___ When I lost hope, you were there to re - mind ___

At the Beginning - 5 - 1

18

20

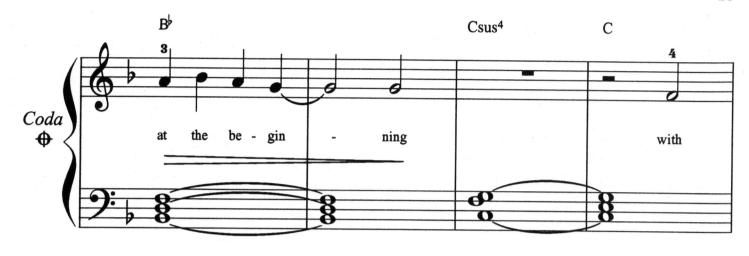

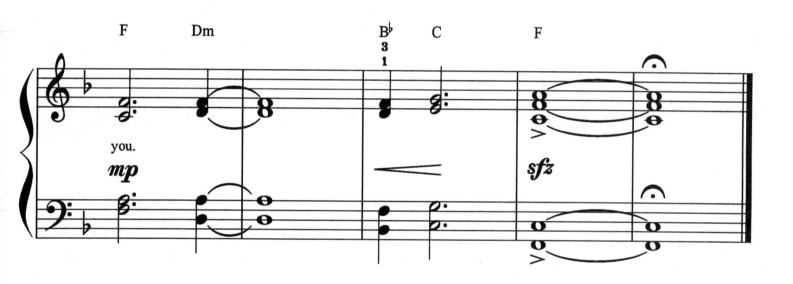

Verse 3:
We were strangers
On a crazy adventure,
Never dreaming
How our dream would come true.
Now here we stand
Unafraid of the future,
At the beginning with you.
(To Chorus:)

From the Touchstone Motion Picture "CON AIR"

HOW DO I LIVE

Words and Music by
DIANE WARREN
Arranged by DAN COATES

Moderately slow

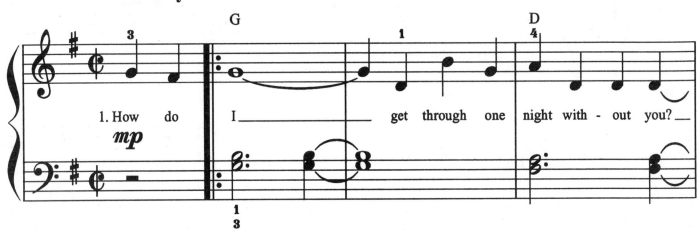

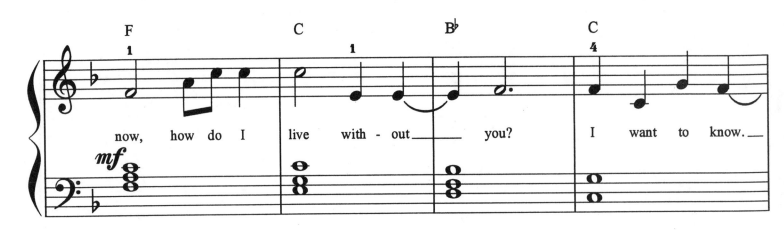

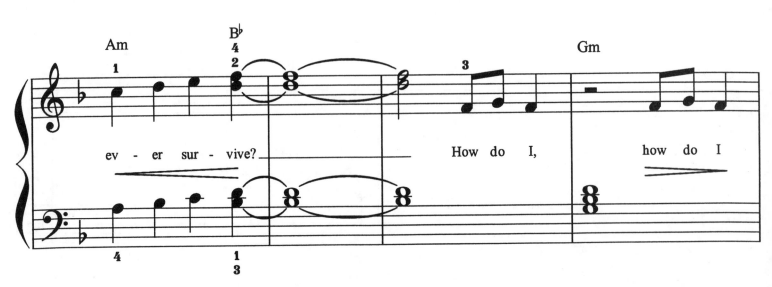

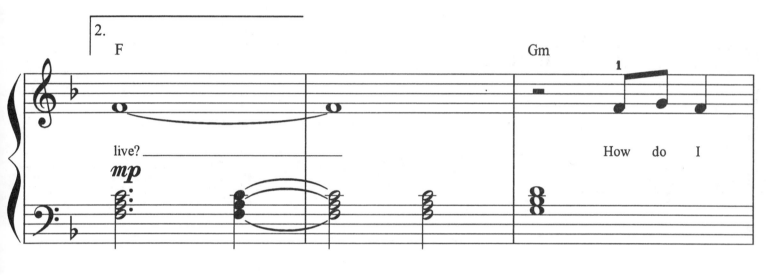

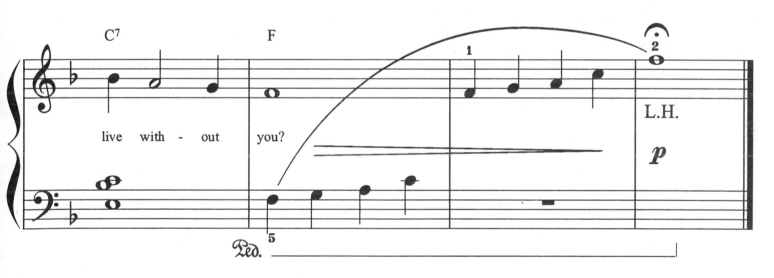

Verse 2:
Without you, there'd be no sun up in my sky,
There would be no love in my life,
There'd be no world left for me.
And I, baby, I don't know what I would do,
I'd be lost if I lost you.
If you ever leave,
Baby, you would take away everything
Real in my life.
And tell me now...
(To Chorus:)

I BELIEVE I CAN FLY

Words and Music by
R. KELLY
Arranged by DAN COATES

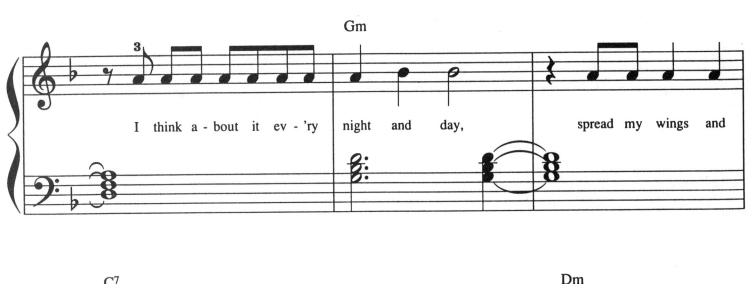

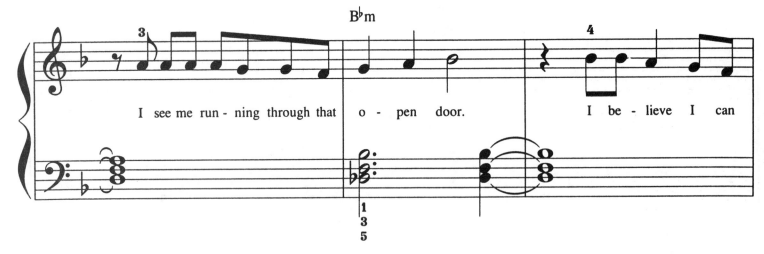

From the Motion Picture "THE PREACHER'S WIFE"

I BELIEVE IN YOU AND ME

Words and Music by
SANDY LINZER and DAVID WOLFERT
Arranged by DAN COATES

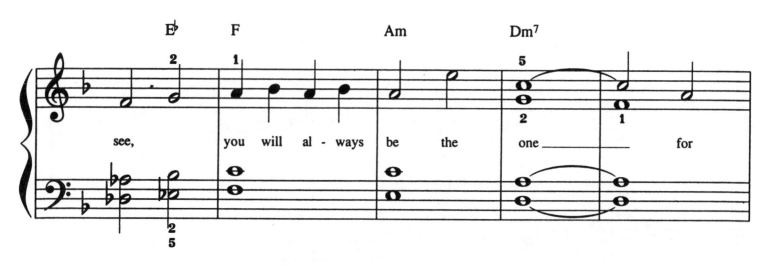

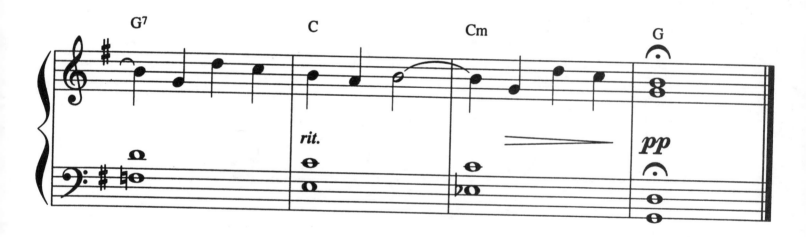

Verse 2:
I will never leave you side,
I will never hurt your pride.
When all the chips are down,
I will always be around
Just to be right where you are, my love.
Oh, I love you, boy.
I will never leave you out,
I will always let you in
To places no one has ever been.
Deep inside, can't you see?
I believe in you and me.

From the Motion Picture "THE MIRROR HAS TWO FACES"

I FINALLY FOUND SOMEONE

Words and Music by
BARBRA STREISAND, MARVIN HAMLISCH,
R.J. LANGE and BRYAN ADAMS
Arranged by DAN COATES

I Finally Found Someone - 5 - 1

From Touchstone Pictures' "ARMAGEDDON"

I DON'T WANT TO MISS A THING

Words and Music by
DIANE WARREN
Arranged by DAN COATES

I just wan - na hold you close, feel your heart so close to mine,

_ and just stay here in this mo - ment for all the rest of time. _

Ba - by, ba - by. _

I SAY A LITTLE PRAYER

Words by
HAL DAVID

Music by
BURT BACHARACH
Arranged by DAN COATES

Brightly

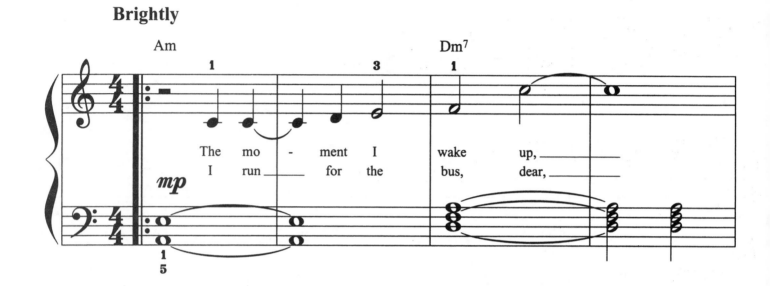

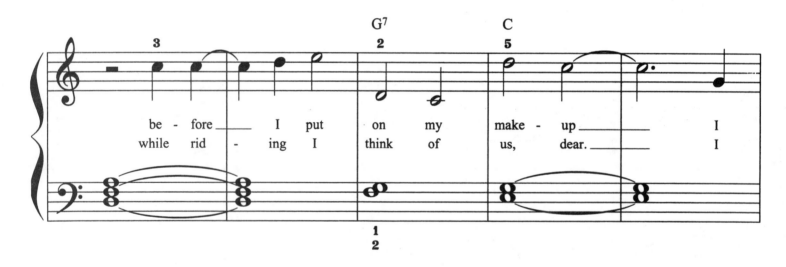

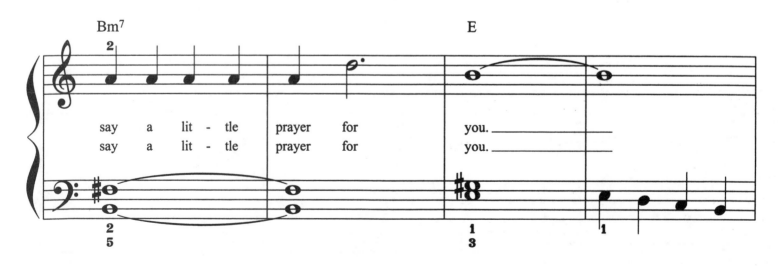

47

I Say a Little Prayer - 4 - 4

From the Twentieth Century Fox Motion Picture "ANASTASIA"

JOURNEY TO THE PAST

Lyrics by
LYNN AHRENS

Music by
STEPHEN FLAHERTY
Arranged by DAN COATES

Not too fast

50

52

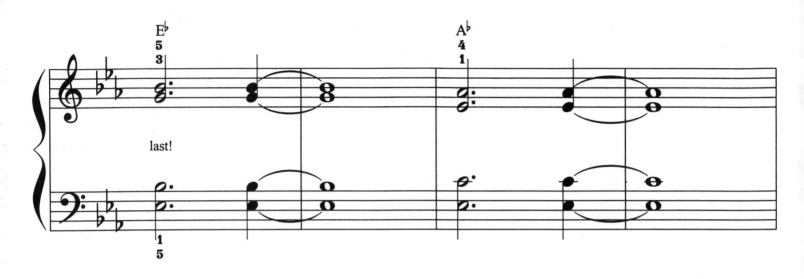

last!

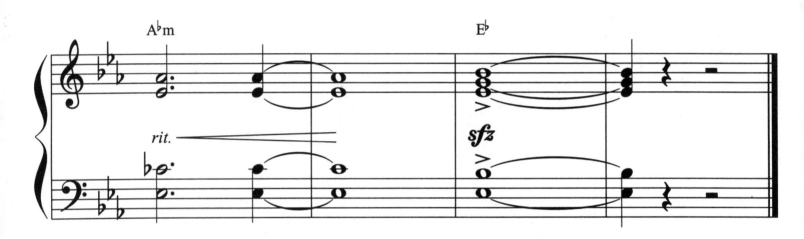

rit.

sfz

Verse 3:
One step at a time.
One hope, then another.
Who knows where this road may go.
Back to who I was.
On to find my future.
Things my heart still needs to know.
(To Coda:)

From Warner Bros. "QUEST FOR CAMELOT"

LOOKING THROUGH YOUR EYES

Words and Music by
CAROLE BAYER SAGER
and DAVID FOSTER
Arranged by DAN COATES

Moderately slow

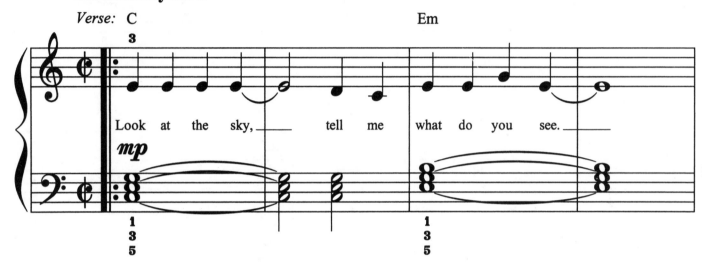

Look at the sky, ____ tell me what do you see. ____

Just close your eyes ____ and de - scribe it to me. ____ The

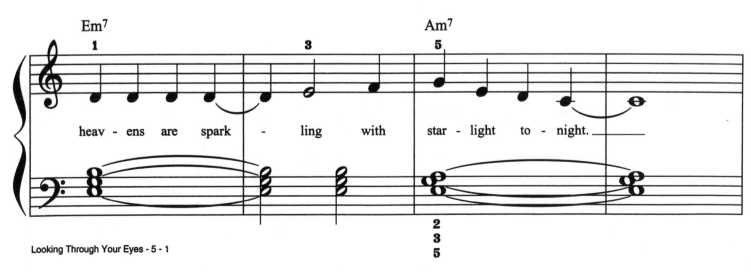

heav - ens are spark - ling with star - light to - night. ____

Looking Through Your Eyes - 5 - 1

54

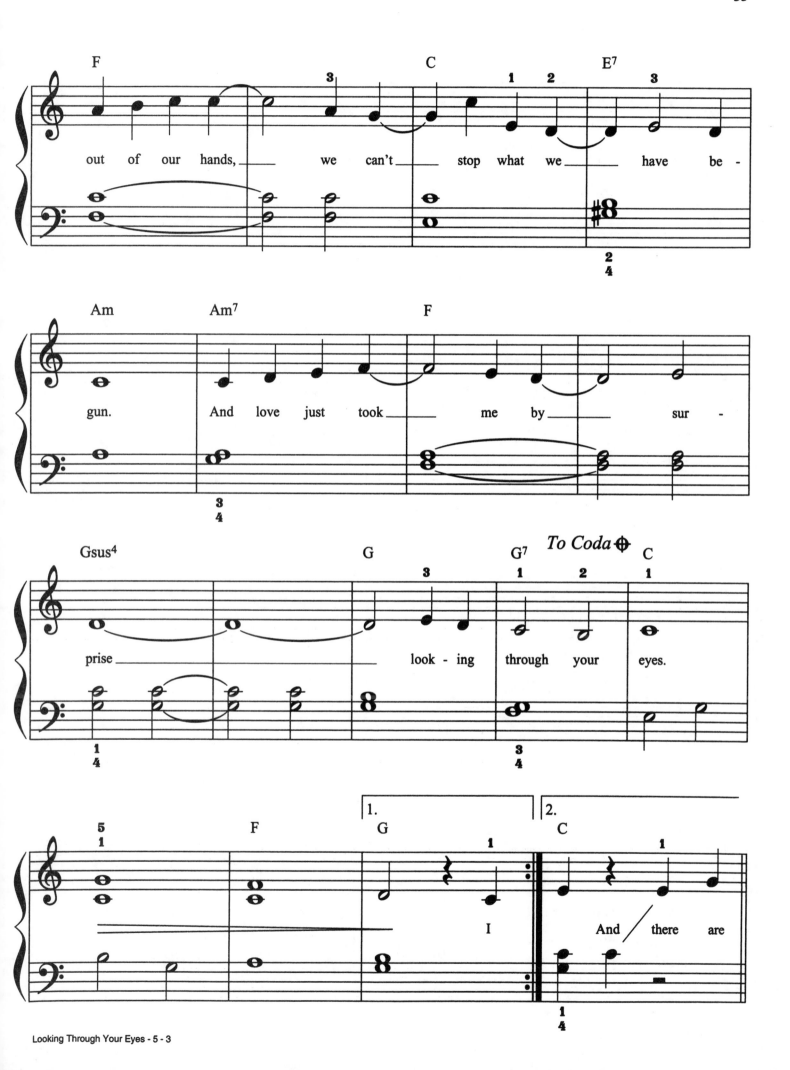

Verse 2:
I see the heavens each time that you smile.
I hear your heartbeat just go on for miles,
And suddenly I know why life is worthwhile.
That's what I see through your eyes.
(To Chorus:)

Verse 3:
I look at myself and instead I see us.
Wherever I am now, it feels like enough.
And I see a girl who is learning to trust.
That's what I see through your eyes.
(To Chorus:)

MY ONE TRUE FRIEND
(From "ONE TRUE THING")

Words and Music by
CAROLE BAYER SAGER, CAROLE KING
and DAVID FOSTER
Arranged by DAN COATES

Slowly, with expression

60

ONCE UPON A DREAM
(From Walt Disney's "SLEEPING BEAUTY")

Words and Music by
SAMMY FAIN and JACK LAWRENCE
Arranged by DAN COATES

Moderate waltz tempo

Once Upon a Dream - 3 - 1

From the Twentieth Century-Fox Motion Picture "STAR WARS"

STAR WARS
(Main Title)

Music by
JOHN WILLIAMS
Arranged by DAN COATES

Star Wars - 3 - 1

Paramount Pictures Presents a Lorimar-Martin Elfand Production-a Taylor Hackford Film
''AN OFFICER AND A GENTLEMAN''

UP WHERE WE BELONG
(From the Motion Picture ''An Officer and a Gentleman'')

Words by
WILL JENNINGS

Music by
JACK NITZSCHE and BUFFY SAINTE-MARIE
Arranged by DAN COATES

D.S. 𝄋 al Coda

Coda

Up Where We Belong - 3 - 3

THAT THING YOU DO!

Words and Music by
ADAM SCHLESINGER
Arranged by DAN COATES

Bright rock tempo

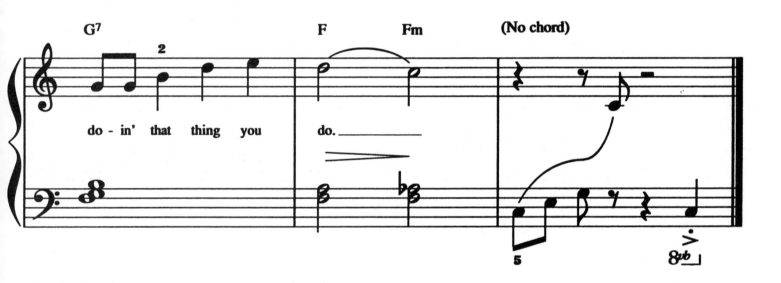

Verse 2:
I know all the games you play.
And I'm gonna find a way to let you know
That you'll be mine someday.
'Cause we could be happy, can't you see?
If you'd only let me be the one to hold you
And keep you here with me.
'Cause I try and try to forget you, girl,
But it's just too hard to do.
Every time you do that thing you do.

Verse 3:
(8 Bar Instrumental Solo...)
'Cause we could be happy, can't you see?
If you'd only let me be the one to hold you
And keep you here with me.
'Cause it hurts me so just to see you go
Around with someone new.
(To Coda:)

From the Warner Bros. Motion Picture ''BEST FRIENDS''

HOW DO YOU KEEP THE MUSIC PLAYING?

Words by
ALAN and MARILYN BERGMAN

Music by
MICHEL LEGRAND
Arranged by DAN COATES

Slowly, with feeling

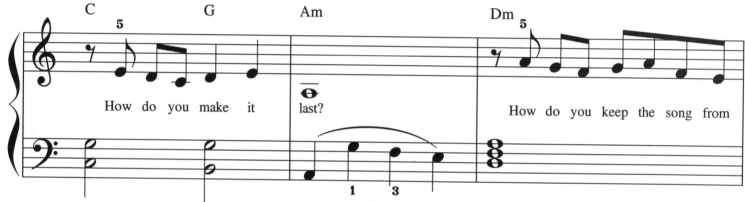

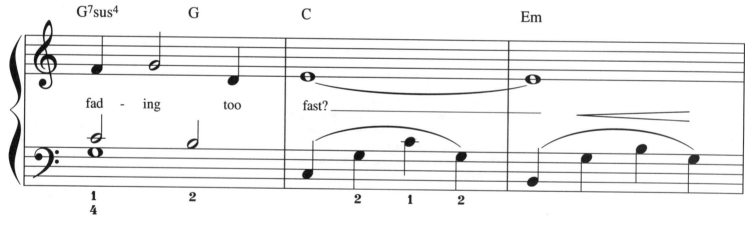

How Do You Keep the Music Playing? - 4 - 1

BECAUSE YOU LOVED ME
(Theme from "Up Close & Personal")

Words and Music by
DIANE WARREN
Arranged by DAN COATES

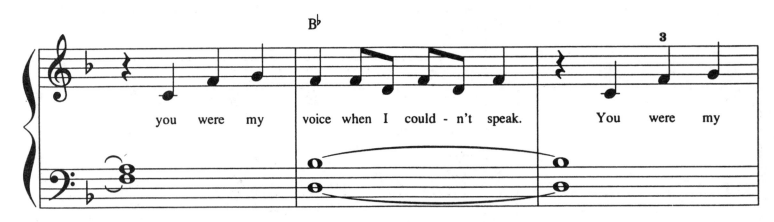

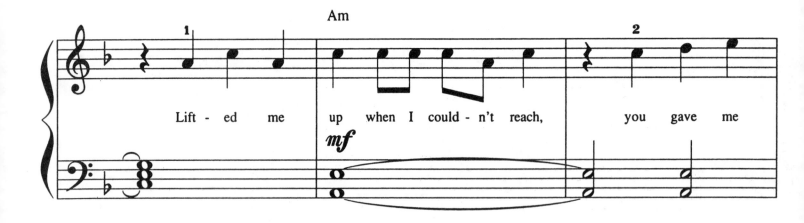

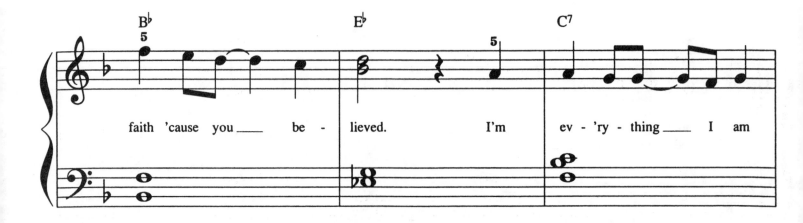

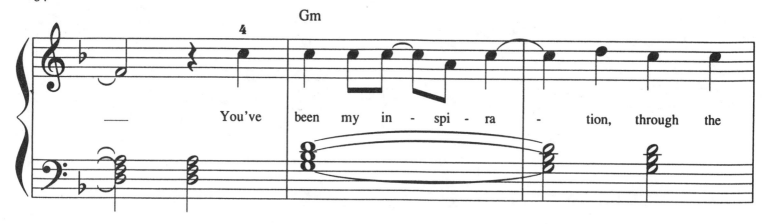

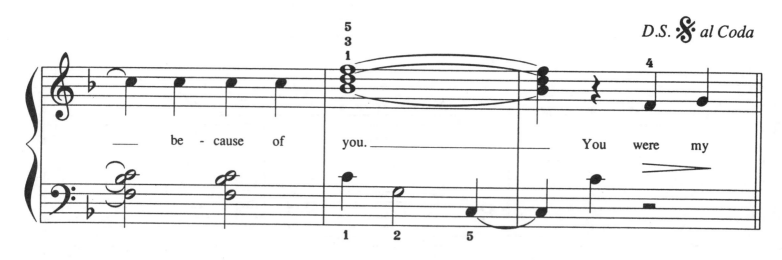

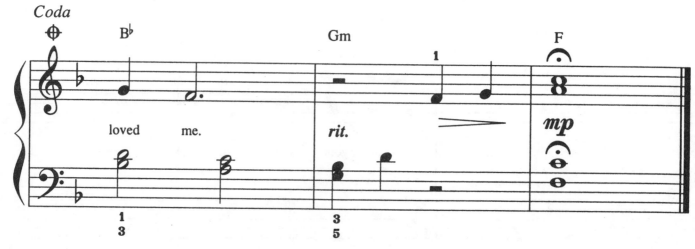